HARMONIC ENCOUNTERS

Unveiling the Melody Within

Dr. Renée D. Charles, PhD

ISBN: 978-1-7338174-8-6

Published by Elite International Publishing

Marietta, Georgia 30066, USA

Library of Congress Control Number: Pending

Dedication

To the artists who became landmarks in my inner world—not simply heard, but felt—
as if each song left a fingerprint on my nervous system,
each chorus a small instruction in how to survive, how to soften, how to return.

To Chaka Khan, for voice as power, emotion as precision, and freedom as sound—whose fire, range, and undeniable presence taught me that power can be both polished and raw, and that strength can sing without asking permission.

To Fred Hammond, for lyrics with divine meaning, harmony that heals, rhythm that carries faith, and music that steadies the spirit—whose worship and lyrical honesty strengthened me across seasons, reminding my soul what it means to be held and helping me believe again in the restoring work of harmony.

To Stevie Wonder, for musical genius that transcends limitations and reminds us that vision is more than sight—and that music is timeless; songs in the keys of life, where joy and truth can live in the same chord.

To Luther Vandross, for the tenderness in your tone, the precision in your phrasing, and the velvet honesty that made love sound like a language the body understands—teaching me that softness can be strength, and that intimacy has rhythm.

To Jonathan Reynolds, for emotional architecture—music that created space to feel, reflect, and return to self and to God; a sound that carried messages I needed before I had language for them—melodies that felt like guidance when I didn't yet know what to call it.

To Kendrick Lamar, for lyrical courage, truth-telling, and the fearless use of sound as social consciousness; whose social messages—delivered with lyrical precision and fearless honesty—remind us that music can carry truth, hold tension, and still move people toward healing; language that refuses to look away, making honesty rhythmic when silence would be easier.

To Diana Ross—from my childhood—for style, couture fashion, versatility, tenacity, and life force I embodied long before I had language for influence; for helping me imagine what it looks like to embody presence, and for showing me—early—what presence looks like when it walks into a room.

This book is, in many ways, a thank you.
This is my gratitude made audible.

Because across the seasons, you didn't just give the world songs—you helped shape the music within me, and helped me recognize my own.

FRAMEWORK STATEMENT

A Model for Emotional Coherence

This is not just a book.
It is a framework.
It is a score.

Harmonic Encounters is a structured way of understanding how sound, rhythm, belief, and lived experience shape identity, behavior, and healing.

But more than structure, it is an invitation to listen.

To recognize that your life is not random—it is composed.
That your responses carry rhythm.
That your relationships move in timing.
That your body holds tone long before language forms meaning.

This work emerges from years of observation, lived experience, and professional practice—refined over time into a language that could hold what words often miss. What you will encounter here is not simply theory, but a framework shaped through pattern recognition, embodiment, internal awareness, and conceptual continuity. These insights were not formed in a single moment, but revealed over time—through listening, practice, and lived integration. And while language can be supported by many tools, the depth of integration required to sustain this kind of continuity across an entire body of work is not something that can be artificially generated. It must be lived, recognized, and translated with intention.

Understanding the Model

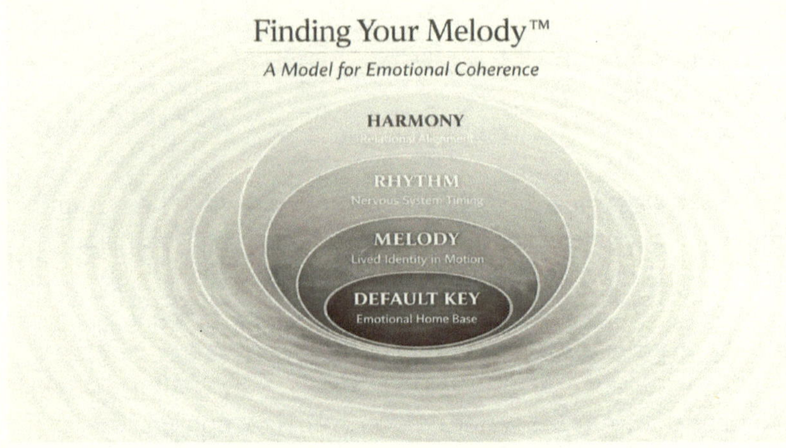

Figure 1. Harmonic Encounters Model

Before moving forward, take a moment to notice the structure you are about to engage.

The *Finding Your Melody*™ model is not meant to be memorized. It is meant to be recognized.

It reflects how human experience organizes itself—through layers of pattern, response, and meaning.

At the center is what I call your **default key**, the emotional home base your body returns to without conscious thought. This is where many of your automatic responses begin.

Surrounding that is your **melody**, your lived identity in motion. The way you move through the world is shaped by experience, expression, and internal narrative.

Beyond that is **rhythm**, the timing of your nervous system. The pace at which you respond, regulate, and engage with what is happening around you.

And finally, **harmony**, your relational alignment. How your internal state meets the external world, and how connection, tension, and repair are experienced.

These are not separate parts.
They are layered expressions of the same system.

As you move through this book, you will begin to recognize where you are in the model—not by analysis, but by awareness.

You are not learning something new.
You are learning how to hear what has always been present.

Chapter 1

Harmonic Encounters: The World Is Teeming with Melody

Before understanding arrives, notice what your body already knows.

This chapter introduces the foundation of the Harmonic Encounters framework—not only as a concept, but as a listening posture, where rhythm, tone, and internal signal begin to come into awareness.

A song finds you before you ask for it—like it was already on its way.

You are folding laundry. Driving. Standing in a checkout line. And suddenly a melody rises inside you as if someone pressed play beneath your ribs.

You may not know the name of it.
You may not remember when you first heard it. Yet your body responds.

Your throat tightens.

Your shoulders soften.
Your breath shifts.
Your eyes warm.

The mind begins searching for an explanation. The body has already recognized something.

I remember my grandmother humming long before I understood what she was doing. There was no radio playing.
No performance.
No audience.

Just her moving through the house, and that sound. It wasn't a tune I could identify.
It wasn't a hymn I could name.

One day I asked her, "What song is that?" She smiled gently and said,
"It's not a song I know. It's something the Lord downloaded into my spirit."
She was not trying to remember. She was not trying to impress.
She was not even trying to sing. She was responding.

Her body already knew something her mind did not need to translate. That was my first harmonic encounter.

We are making music every moment.
Through tone, timing, silence, breath, word choice, posture, reaction, restraint.

Sometimes we are in key. Sometimes we are out of key.

And discordant notes do not harmonize—not with our inner voice,
and not with others operating on different frequencies.

This is not metaphor alone.
This is lived neuroscience and lived spirituality.

This is a human story about how sound, rhythm, and vibration shape identity, emotion, choice, and connection.

Music becomes the universal language of the emotional self.

And neuroscience simply explains why what we already know feels true. Your

essence is a melody.

When you have presence and walk into a room, people hear it—even before you speak.

Presence is a clear note.
When you walk in presence, the air shifts. The room makes space—
the way a cymbal announces itself and everything else adjusts.

You do not force attention.
You do not demand accommodation. The atmosphere responds.

This is not charisma.
It is coherence.

When your inner rhythm aligns with your outer expression, the signal is clear. And clarity has sound.

While writing Quantum Nexus, a thought emerged that would not leave me: what you are looking for is looking for you.
I thought of that childhood scene from E.T.—how a small trail of sweetness was left out, not realizing that both parties were searching for each other.[1]

One believed he was seeking. The other believed he was lost.

Neither knew they were already moving toward mutual recognition. The

sweetness was not manipulation.
It was signal.

Sometimes a melody arrives not to entertain you,
but to lead you back to something already searching for you. A song that "just

shows up" is not random.

It can be a trail left by something already in motion—a memory seeking integration,
a truth looking for language,
a part of you asking to be retrieved, a frequency trying to reconnect.

What we often look for wants to be found—
but the lost and the seeker are resonating at different frequencies and emitting a different song.

So they pass each other.

Not because the answer is absent,
but because the signal has not yet aligned. Then one day, a melody appears.

And without knowing why, you follow it.

Not because you understand it.
Because your nervous system recognizes it. Something found me.

Or perhaps…
we finally recognized each other. The world teems with melody.

Everything carries a signature: notes, tones, rhythms, patterns.

Even your language has music—cadence, pitch, pauses, emphasis. Even your silence has tone.

We do not only communicate through what we say. We communicate through how we sound,
how we time our words,
and what our presence plays in the room.

Two people can share the same conversation and leave with entirely different

internal experiences. One heard harmony.
The other heard dissonance.

One felt safe.
The other felt threat.

The difference is rare in the facts. It is in the frequency.

Music is spiritual by nature—not because it belongs to a doctrine, but because it moves through what is seen and unseen. It shapes emotions, organizes memory, regulates the nervous system, and connects people across languages and cultures.

The brain does not process music as information first. It processes it as a signal.

Which is why the song often arrives before the explanation. Which is why the body reacts before meaning forms.
Which is why tears come before the story.

Neuroscience will name salience, predictive timing, memory networks. Lived experience says something simpler:

I was found.

Chapter 2

The Body Hears First: Frequency, Safety, and the Survival Brain

Some rhythms were learned before language. This chapter listens for them.

Before the mind interprets meaning, the body registers sound. A tone can soothe you or startle you.
A melody can loosen your jaw or tighten your chest.
A voice can feel like home—or like danger—without saying a single threatening word.

This is not imagination.
It is the nervous system listening.

We often tell ourselves we respond to content.
But so much of what we call "communication" happens before content arrives.

It happens in timing

In intensity.
In the emotional contour of a voice.
In what the body senses underneath the words.

Your body hears first.
Your mind explains later.

There are moments when someone says the right words, yet your body does not soften. And there are moments when very few words are spoken—and you feel safe anyway.

Sometimes safety is not in the sentence. It is in the sound.

A steady tone.
A gentle tempo.
A pause that doesn't punish.
A voice that doesn't rush your nervous system. And sometimes the opposite is

true.

A sharp edge.
A clipped rhythm.
A volume that feels too close.
A tone that carries an old threat into a new room.

You may not be able to prove it.
You may not even be able to name it.

But your body has already formed a conclusion.

There is a part of you designed to respond faster than language.

The brainstem—often called the survival brain—supports rapid orientation: arousal, startle, protective reflexes. It reacts to patterns and intensities long before you assemble a coherent narrative.

The amygdala, often associated with the emotional brain, acts like an internal alarm and relevance detector. It scans for what feels important, especially what feels threatening or meaningful. It does not ask for evidence. It asks, "Is this safe? Does this matter?"

The cortex, particularly the prefrontal cortex—the executive or "smart" brain—helps you reason, interpret, regulate, and decide. It gives context. It slows the story down. It asks, "What is really happening?"

But here is the sequence that matters:

The emotional brain reacts. The executive brain explains.

When a sound pattern resembles something once linked to fear, your system can mobilize before you remember why. By the time your cortex forms a sentence, your body has already chosen a posture.

That is why you can "know" you are safe yet feel unsafe. That is why you can forgive yet still flinch.
That is why a song can change your state in seconds.

You are not unstable.
You are patterned.

Some songs evoke a response because the sound activates a painful memory. Other songs return you to joy—time and space—where safety lived in your muscles.

A chorus can evoke tears without a story attached. Not because you are dramatic—
but because the body is recalling a state, not a sentence.

The mind wants a clear explanation.
The body often answers in sensation instead: warmth behind the eyes, heaviness in the chest, a throat that tightens,

a breath that shortens,
a sudden calm that feels like permission.

Words demand logic, readiness, and interpretation. Music offers recognition, safety, and timing.

The brain does not process music as information first. It processes it as a signal.

That's why the song arrives before the explanation. The body reacts before meaning forms.
Tears come before the story.

Neuroscience can call it salience, memory networks, predictive timing. But lived experience says something simpler:

Something found me.

Chapter 3

You Are a Song: Notes, Keys, Rhythm, and Construction

What we call silence often carries the loudest instruction.

A song is not only a melody. It is a construction.

Rhythm (time). Melody (lead line).
Harmony (supporting chords). Dynamics (volume).
Silence (space).
And sometimes lyrics—meaning carried by language.

When you understand song construction, you begin to understand self-construction. Because whether you know it or not, you are already making music:

in how you enter a room, in how you answer,
in how you pause, in what you soften,

in what you emphasize, in what you refuse to say.

There is a reason some titles land like truth before they land like art. Stevie Wonder's *Songs in the Key of Life.* [2]

Not songs about life.
Songs in the keys of life.

Life itself has a key,
and meaning emerges when sound aligns with lived experience.

Rhythm gives predictability. Melody gives identity.
Harmony gives belonging. Dynamics give emotional intensity.
Silence gives meaning, restraint, and room for what cannot be rushed. A key is

an emotional home base.

Some people default to urgency. Some to withdraw.
Some to caretaking, control, humor, silence.

These are not personality quirks.
They are often adaptive rhythms—learned ways of staying safe, staying seen, staying intact.

Rhythm is the pace of life. Fast. Slow.
Interruptive. Flowing.
Predictable. Syncopated.

Rhythm mirrors nervous system state. Melody is the human through-line.

A humming grandmother moving through the house with no need to name the song. A melody that appears uninvited, like a message you didn't request. A voice that steadies you without explaining. A sound that carries you back to yourself.

Harmony surrounds the melody.
In life, harmony is relational: supporting voices, shared timing, safe resonance, and repair when the song gets disrupted.

Dynamics are not only about volume. They are emotional force.

Silence is not absence.

Silence is space.

The brain anticipates what comes next based on patterns—timing, tone,

sequence, repetition. When timing is consistent, the nervous system relaxes. When timing is chaotic, it braces.

You are not trapped in one arrangement. You can change tempo.
You can modulate.
You can learn new timing.
You can return your key.

And when you do, you stop forcing your life to sound like someone else's song.
You begin to live until your inner rhythm matches your outward life—and your presence becomes coherent.

Not because you are louder. Because you are true.

Chapter 4

Memory Has a Soundtrack: Implicit Memory and Musical Recall

Emotion moves faster than explanation. Music knows why.

A single chorus can return you to a room you haven't entered in decades—not because you decided to remember, but because music carried you there.

This is why music is both comfort and confrontation.
It retrieves states, not just scenes.

Research suggests that memory is not simply recalled—it is reconstructed. Each time you remember, certain elements are strengthened while others fade. In that moment of recall, memory becomes flexible—capable of updating—before it stabilizes again. The hippocampus supports this process, working in concert with broader neural networks that store meaning and association.

But not all memory arrives with a story.

Implicit memory is the emotional imprint the body carries—often without language. A song can activate grief, longing, or peace even when you cannot name the source. That does not make you unstable. It makes you human.

The body does not wait for explanation.
It responds to pattern, tone, and familiarity.

This is why a melody can soften you before you understand it.
Why your breath can shift before you form a thought.
Why tears can come before you have language to explain them.

The mind looks for sequence—what happened, when, and why.
The body recognizes something else:
Have I felt this before?

And when the answer is yes, the response is already in motion.

Music becomes a bridge between what is known and what has been carried without words. It does not ask you to explain yourself before it reaches you. It meets you where you are—often before you know where that is.

There are songs that comfort because they return you to safety.
There are songs that confront because they return you to something unresolved.

Both are forms of remembering.

Not remembering as narrative—
but remembering as state.

And within that state, something important happens.

Memory, when reactivated, is not fixed. It becomes momentarily open—capable of being experienced differently, interpreted differently, held differently. What once felt overwhelming can be encountered with new awareness. What once lived only in reaction can begin to move toward meaning.

This is not about rewriting the past.
It is about changing how the past lives in you.

Music reaches what words cannot always express.
It retrieves what has been held beneath explanation.

And in that retrieval, there is a possibility—
not only to remember,
but to re-author the way the body holds the past.

And when you begin to hear it, you realize—
the song has been remembering you, too.

Chapter 5

What Note Are You Resonating At: Default Keys and Emotional Home Base

The Key You Return To Before You Choose

Within the Harmonic Encounters framework, this is where learned emotional patterns are heard more clearly—revealing the key you have been living in, whether chosen or inherited.

Not one we chose—
one we learned.

A place the body returns to
without asking permission.

Not because it is right.
Because it is familiar.

You may notice it
not in calm moments—
but under pressure.

When the room shifts.
When the tone changes.
When something inside you tightens
before you can name why.

Some move faster.

Words come quickly.
Energy rises.
The need to respond, explain, and resolve
arrives before understanding.

Some go quiet.

Not as peace—
but as a retreat.

A soft disappearance
that feels like safety
but costs presence.

Some adjust.

Tone softens.
Edges smooth.
The room is managed
before the self is heard.

And some stay still.

Watching.
Reading.
Sensing the room
before deciding how to enter it.

These are not personality traits.

They are remembered rhythms.

What you are experiencing here is what neuroscience often describes as a state-dependent response. Under pressure, the brain defaults to previously learned patterns—what I refer to as your emotional key. These patterns are not chosen in the moment; they are activated.

A key is not just emotional.

It is physiological.

It is the place your body returns to
when it does not have time to decide.

And here is what matters:

The key you return to
is not always the key you belong to.

Sometimes what feels like the truth
is simply what has been repeated.

Sometimes what feels urgent
is simply what has been practiced.

Sometimes what feels like you
is only what has been familiar long enough
to feel like home.

But familiarity is not identity.

There are moments
when you enter a room
and everything feels different.

Nothing has changed externally—
yet something in you
is not responding the same way.

You pause
instead of reacting.

You breathe
before speaking.

You listen
without bracing.

That is not performance.

That is modulation.

Not forcing yourself into a new key—
but recognizing
you were never limited to one.

Some of you can carry a tune
but have never asked
What key are you in?

Some of you cannot sing at all—
yet you know
there is a song in you
waiting to be heard.

This chapter is not asking you to change.

It is asking you to listen.

Because once you hear it—
once you recognize
the note you return to without thinking—

you begin to notice
you are not confined to it.

And something shifts.

Not dramatically.
Not all at once.

But enough
for a different note
to enter the song.

And when that happens—

you are no longer reacting
from memory alone.

You are responding
from awareness.

And awareness
has a different sound.

A Harmonic Reflection: "My John"

What you are about to read is not simply a song.

It is an expression of lived experience—where memory, emotion, and rhythm converge.

Within the Harmonic Encounters framework, this reflection illustrates how unresolved emotional patterns continue to carry tone, even across time.

My John

There was a time I was your melody

You played me soft in every key

Saxophone nights and city lights

You saw forever… I saw maybe

You held me like I was already yours

I held the moment, nothing more

You hoped for it… I didn't claim it

You named a future… I couldn't frame it

You loved me loud… I loved the sound

Of being seen when you were around

My John…

You were mine, but not the one I became with

Different planes, but you stayed close

You cheered me on, you loved me most

While I was building something new

You stood in place… steady, true

You gave a love that didn't bend

But I was never meant to end there

If I called you… would time rewind?

Or just remind me of who I was back then… not now, not mine

Two babies born in a dream last night

One I claimed… one stayed in your eyes

You hoped for it… I didn't claim it

Some love is real… but not meant to stay in it

My John…

A song that plays… but never finishes

Within the Harmonic Encounters framework, this reflection reveals how emotional patterns are not always logical—they are rhythmic.

Some connections do not end; they sustain.

And until they are understood, they continue to play beneath conscious awareness.

Chapter 6

Bio-Genetic Syncopation: The Off-Beat Rhythm Written Into Your Cells

When the Body Responds Before the Mind Understands

Not every reaction is out of time.
Some are perfectly aligned with an older score.

There are moments when something in you moves before you can explain it. A response arrives early. A feeling rises without warning. A reaction forms before thought has time to follow.

It can feel out of place.
Out of proportion.
Out of rhythm.

But what if it isn't?

The phrase *bio-genetic syncopation* did not come to me as language. It came as sound—an off-beat note, unresolved, persistent.

In music, syncopation disrupts expectation. It emphasizes what is usually unaccented. It arrives where you do not anticipate it, and because of that, you feel it more.

I began to recognize the same pattern in the body.

Reactions that seemed early, but were not misplaced.
Emotional rhythms that did not wait for reasoning—but were not without meaning.
Something striking between the beats.

Not randomly.
Precisely.

Long before words are chosen, the body has already remembered.
Not in sentences.
Not in the story.
In rhythm.

What we sometimes call "overreacting" is often a perfectly timed response to an earlier internal score.

A room changes, and something in you shifts.
A tone lands, and your body tightens.
A moment passes—but something in you is already responding to what is not fully visible in the present.

Not because you are confused.
Because you are patterned.

There are rhythms carried through experience, through repetition, through memory. And some may reach even deeper, shaped by what has been lived, endured, and encoded before language ever had the chance to name it.

This is what I call *bio-genetic syncopation.*

Not as a diagnosis.
As recognition.

An understanding that what appears offbeat may be aligned with something older than the moment you are standing in.

Old rhythms in new rooms.

And when the present meets the past in that way, the body does not respond logically.
It responds musically.

Which is why the explanation often comes too late.
The response has already sounded.

But here is what matters:

You are not required to silence that rhythm.
You are invited to listen to it.

Not to remain bound to it—
but to understand what it has been holding.

Because returning is not a betrayal of what has been.
It is wisdom.

It is the ability to honor what once kept you in rhythm with survival—
while choosing what allows you to live in alignment now.

And when you begin to hear it clearly—
not as noise,
not as disruption,
but as pattern—

something shifts.

You gain something you did not have before.

Not control.
Not suppression.

Choice.

And once you hear it, you are no longer at the mercy of the rhythm—
you are in a relationship with it.

Chapter 7

Think It · Whisper It · Speak It: From Intention to Embodiment

Regulation is not control. It is attunement.

There are moments when something forms inside you before you have words for it. It does not arrive as language—it arrives as knowing. A quiet awareness. A subtle recognition that something is present, even if it has not yet taken shape.

That is the beginning.

Thinking is not just cognition.
It is where meaning gathers.

It is where something begins to organize itself within you—before it is influenced, before it is interpreted by others, before it is exposed to the world.

But what remains only in thought often stays untested.
Unfelt.
Unlived.

So something in you moves it forward.

Not into declaration—
but into sound.

You whisper it.

Not for the room.
Not for performance.
But for yourself.

This is the first crossing:

internal → semi-external

The whisper is subtle, but it matters. It allows the body to meet what the mind has already formed. It introduces breath, vibration, and presence. It lets you hear what you have been holding—without the pressure of being heard.

And something happens there.

What was once abstract begins to take form.
What was once internal begins to reorganize.

This is where change begins to anchor.

Because transformation is not created at the moment of speaking.
It is shaped in the movement that precedes it.

This is where the internal pattern begins to shift. Meaning is no longer held in its original form. It begins to reorganize—subtly, but significantly—before it is ever expressed. You begin to experience it differently.
Not because the past has changed—
but because your relationship with it is beginning to shift.

And when it settles—when it no longer feels foreign, when it no longer feels like something you are trying to convince yourself of—you move again.

This time, into voice.

semi-external → fully expressed

You speak it.

And when you do, it lands differently.

Not forced.
Not rehearsed.
Not defensive.

It carries weight because it has already moved through you.

There are times when we bypass this movement.

We think something—and immediately say it—without allowing the body to meet it. Without allowing it to settle. Without allowing it to become ours.

And when that happens, the words may sound right,
but something underneath them feels unstable.

Not because the words are wrong—
but because they have not been integrated.

There are also times when we remain in thought.

We think, and think, and think—
but never allow the sound to form.

And what is true remains internal.
Unspoken.
Unclaimed.
Unlived.

There is wisdom in the movement:

internal → semi-external → fully expressed

Not as a rule—
but as a rhythm.

And within that rhythm, something deeper is happening.

Thought becomes sound.
Sound becomes experience.
Experience begins to reshape meaning.

This is how internal patterns change—not through force, but through alignment.

When you move with that rhythm, something stabilizes.

Your voice steadies.
Your breath supports you.
Your body no longer resists what you are saying.

Your words no longer feel like something you are trying to hold together.
They feel like something you are standing in.

Because your voice is not only a means of communication.
It is regulation.
It is identity.
It is a frequency made audible.

And when what you think, what you feel, and what you say move together—without interruption, without contradiction—you are no longer trying to be heard.

You are already aligned.

Think It · Whisper It · Speak It™ is an original framework introduced in this work. Related neuroscience concepts are referenced to explain underlying mechanisms, not to claim the origin of the method or its sequencing.

Chapter 8

Dissonance Is Not Always Destruction: Discernment and Staying in Key

Healing does not erase rhythm. It changes tempo.

Dissonance Is Information

Dissonance is not silence.

A chord that does not resolve.
A tone that lands without harmony.
A tension that does not settle.

Not everything that feels off
is wrong.

But it is saying something.

There is a moment—
subtle, often missed—

when you recognize
the song has shifted.

Not with panic.
Not with urgency.

But with knowing.

Something is out of key.

Discernment does not rush to correct.

It listens.

It notices
what belongs
and what does not.

What is aligned
and what is forcing itself to sound like it is.

Sometimes, what you feel is discomfort.
It is not dangerous.

It is different.

A pause that didn't land.
A word that carried another tone beneath it.
A rhythm that moved too quickly—or not at all.

And your body knows.

Before language.
Before explanation.

You may feel it as irritation.
As tightening.
As a quiet internal shift
you cannot fully name.

Not because something is wrong.

But because something
is no longer aligned.

Dissonance is not always destruction.

Sometimes it is information—

an invitation
to align what is seen and unseen,
the way countless notes
wait to resolve
into a melody within you.

You do not have to fear that moment.

You do not have to silence it.

If you stay long enough to listen—
without forcing resolution—

something becomes clear.

Not all at once.

But enough.

And clarity has its own sound.

Not loud.
Not urgent.
Not demanding.

Steady.

And in that steadiness,
you find yourself again.

Not reacting to the noise—
but responding
to what is true.

Chapter 9

Harmonic Relationships: Resonance, Repair, and Creative Alignment

Collaboration: What was once survival can become expression.

Harmony is not negotiated.

It is recognized.

It begins
when something in you
remembers what alignment feels like.

There are moments
when connection is effortless—

when tone meets tone,
when timing holds,
when nothing has to be explained.

And there are moments
when something shifts.

A word lands wrong.
A pause feels too long.
A response misses its mark.

Not because the relationship is broken—
but because something moved out of key.

What matters is not the moment of disruption.

It is what follows.

Do you force the sound?

Do you withdraw from it?

Or do you listen
long enough
to hear where the alignment was lost?

Because harmony does not come from control.

It comes from return.

Not return to the other person—
return to the original frequency within you.

That place that does not rush,
does not collapse,
does not disappear.

When you return there,
your tone changes.

Your presence steadies.

Your words no longer chase understanding—
they carry it.

And something in the other
can meet you again.

Not because you fixed it.

Because you found your way back
to what was always true.

Harmony is alignment with an intelligent design—
a frequency woven into creation
long before we learned to disrupt it.

And what is formed in coherence
will always seek to return.

Chapter 10

Become the Melody: Alignment, Momentum, and a Life in Harmony

Living in Coherence Without Forcing the Sound

This is where the framework becomes lived experience—not as theory, but as alignment, where your life begins to sound like what is true.

When the melody is restored, the body rests.
By now, you know this book was never only about music.

It was about what music has always been teaching us—quietly, faithfully, through the body.
Life has a key.
Every relationship has a rhythm.
And tone carries truth long before language can defend it.

Harmony is not perfect.
It is alignment—inside yourself first, and then with the world around you.

To become the melody is to stop living as a collection of reactions.
It is to live as a coherent signal.

Alignment is what happens when what you believe, what you practice, and what your body experiences begin to agree.
When your inner rhythm matches your outward life, you stop forcing harmony—you start living it.

Momentum is the natural result of coherence.
Not the frantic momentum of striving, but the kind that feels like flow:

The right conversations arrive.
The right doors open.
Your yes becomes clearer.
Your no becomes cleaner.

Not because life is easy—
but because your frequency is stable.

You have learned to notice dissonance without panic.
You have learned that discomfort can be information.
That discord can be a cue to modulate—not to disappear.
That silence can be wisdom—not punishment.

In earlier chapters, we named the architecture of a song: key, rhythm, melody, harmony, dynamics, and space.

Here is the final translation:

Your key is your emotional home base.
Your rhythm is your nervous system's pace.
Your melody is your authentic line—what returns you to yourself.
Your harmony is relational attunement—the people, practices, and environments that support your signal rather than distort it.

And your presence?

Presence is what happens when you are no longer divided against yourself.
It is not performance.
It is coherence.

When you become the melody, you stop asking the world for permission to sound like yourself.
You listen more closely.
You respond more wisely.
You choose with less noise.

You return to your key—again—until it becomes home.

Because the melody is not only what you sing.
It is how you live.
It is how you love.
It is how you repair.
It is how you walk into rooms without abandoning yourself.

May this book help you hear the song beneath your life—
so you can recognize it, honor it,
and live in harmony with the truth you already carry.

The melody does not end here. It continues in the life you are now choosing to live.

About the Author

Dr. Renée D. Charles, PhD, LCSW-R, is a social psychologist, healthcare executive, licensed clinical social worker, and author whose work lives at the intersection of neuroscience, emotional intelligence, spirituality, and sound.

Her connection to music began early. At the age of five, she studied classical piano, developing a deep appreciation for structure, tone, and expression. As a vocalist, she performed with a girls' group, toured with local music ensembles, and sang in the Shekinah church choir—experiences that shaped her understanding of music as more than art, but as a lived and embodied language.

She is the Founder, President, and CEO of The Center for Rapid Recovery, Inc., a nonprofit behavioral healthcare organization committed to eliminating racial and ethnic disparities in health and healthcare.

Through her work as a consultant, coach, and speaker, Dr. Charles helps individuals and organizations understand the relationship between thought, emotion, and internal rhythms—guiding transformation through alignment, awareness, and intentional living.

Connect with Dr. Renée D. Charles

Website
www.DrReneeCharles.com

Email
Contact@drreneedcharles.com

Facebook
https://facebook.com/DRRDCPHD

Instagram
@dr_renee_charles

X (Twitter)
@drreneecharles

Other Works by Dr. Renée D. Charles

Published

From Sacrifice to Service

Remembering the Trauma and Healing It

Remembering the Trauma Self Help Workbook (companion workbook,

2019) Know Thyself, Know Thy Brain, Know Thy God

Forthcoming / Title Reserved

Quantum Nexus: What You Are Looking For Is Looking For You (title reserved with the Library of Congress)

References

Janata, P. (2009). The neural architecture of music-evoked autobiographical memories. *Cerebral Cortex*.

Koelsch, S. (2014). Brain correlates of music-evoked emotions. *Nature Reviews Neuroscience*.

LeDoux, J. (1996). *The Emotional Brain: The Mysterious Underpinnings of Emotional Life*. Simon & Schuster.

Moore, B. C. J. (Multiple editions). *An Introduction to the Psychology of Hearing*. Academic Press.

Nader, K., & Hardt, O. (2009). A single standard for memory: The case for reconsolidation. *Nature Reviews Neuroscience*.

Patel, A. D. (2008). *Music, Language, and the Brain*. Oxford University Press.

Panksepp, J. (1998). *Affective Neuroscience: The Foundations of Human and Animal Emotions*. Oxford University Press.

Salimpoor, V. N., Benovoy, M., Larcher, K., Dagher, A., & Zatorre, R. J. (2011). Anatomically distinct dopamine release during the anticipation and experience of peak emotion to music. *Nature Neuroscience*.

Scoville, W. B., & Milner, B. (1957). Loss of recent memory after bilateral hippocampal lesions. *Journal of Neurology, Neurosurgery & Psychiatry*.

Squire, L. R., & Kandel, E. R. (2009). *Memory: From Mind to Molecules* (2nd ed.). Roberts & Company.

Thaut, M. H. (Multiple works). Rhythmic auditory stimulation and entrainment in rehabilitation and performance.
(See the author's clinical research on rhythmic auditory stimulation.)

Wonder, S. (1976). *Songs in the Key of Life* [Album]. Motown Records.

E.T. the Extra-Terrestrial (1982) [Film]. Universal Pictures.

www.ingramcontent.com/pod-product-compliance
Lightning Source LLC
LaVergne TN
LVHW051022080826
845145LV00009B/2748

* 9 7 8 1 7 3 3 8 1 7 4 8 6 *